party food

simple and delicious easy-to-make recipes

Bernice Hurst

p

This is a Parragon Publishing Book
This edition published in 2002

Parragon Publishing
Queen Street House
4 Queen Street
Bath BA1 1HE
United Kingdom

ISBN: 0-75258-717-X

Printed in China

Produced by The Bridgewater Book Company Ltd

Creative Director Terry Jeavons
Art Director Sarah Howerd
Editorial Director Fiona Biggs
Senior Editor Mark Truman
Editorial Assistants Simon Bailey, Tom Kitch
Photographer Ian Parsons
Home Economist Sara Hesketh
Page Make-up Chris and Jane Lanaway

COVER
Photographer Ian Parsons
Home Economist Sara Hesketh

NOTES FOR THE READER

- This book uses both metric and imperial measurements. Follow the same units of measurement throughout; do not mix metric and imperial.
- All spoon measurements are level: teaspoons are assumed to be 5 ml, and tablespoons are assumed to be 15 ml.
- Unless otherwise stated, milk is assumed to be full fat, eggs and individual vegetables such as potatoes are medium, and pepper is freshly ground black pepper.
- Recipes using raw or very lightly cooked eggs should be avoided by infants, the elderly, pregnant women, convalescents, and anyone suffering from an illness.
- Optional ingredients, variations or serving suggestions have not been included in the calculations. The times given are an approximate guide only. Preparation times differ according to the techniques used by different people and the cooking times vary as a result of the type of oven used.

contents

introduction

Nibbling snacks, starters, or canapés offers a particular satisfaction that eating formal knife-and-fork food can't beat. As in countries where large dishes are shared and dipped into with fingers or chunks of bread, most of us instinctively revert to eating with our hands whenever the opportunity arises.

Modern barbecues generally feature food that can be picked up and eaten instantly—burgers, spare ribs, chicken pieces, anything on a stick.

The short time allocated for lunch when at work or school, or the pleasure of a picnic on a warm summer's day, lend themselves to pies, tarts, and pastries, not to mention encouraging creativity in sandwich making. Filling a crusty roll or baguette, or thick slices of fresh bread, with whatever combinations come to hand, makes a delicious and frequently nutritious way of pleasurably satisfying the appetite.

Our party food recipes are suitable for all sorts of occasions. They are good enough to serve to guests and equally suitable for lunch boxes or casual family lunches and suppers. Many are fine on their own, but a combination, served all at once in the style of a Middle Eastern mezze, makes for even more fun.

guide to recipe key		
	easy	Recipes are graded as follows: 1 pea = easy; 2 peas = very easy; 3 peas = extremely easy.
	serves 4	Recipes generally serve four people. Simply halve the ingredients to serve two, taking care not to mix imperial and metric measurements.
	15 minutes	Preparation time. Where chilling food is involved, the necessary time has been added on separately: eg, 15 minutes + 30 minutes to chill.
	15 minutes	Cooking time.

vegetable cream dip
page 16

stuffed tomatoes
page 32

goat cheese & chive croûtons
page 50

chorizo & olive frittata
page 66

dips & spreads

Dips and spreads are simple, versatile fast food. Raw vegetables and crisps taste great with Easy Onion Dip, Hummus, Taramasalata, or Guacamole. And Smoked Fish Pâté or Grandma's Chopped Herring spread lavishly on toast or crackers makes a brilliant lunch or light supper—or even the first course of a special dinner. You can also pack little tubs into a picnic or lunch box for a delicious portable banquet—the possibilities are endless.

hummus

		ingredients	
	easy	1 cup dried garbanzo beans	GARNISH
		cold water, to cover	1 tbsp olive oil
	serves 4	3–6 tbsp lemon juice	1 tsp cayenne pepper or paprika
		3–6 tbsp water	1 tbsp chopped fresh parsley
		2–3 garlic cloves, peeled and crushed	or cilantro
	15 minutes + 1 hour to chill	scant ⅔ cup tahini	
		salt	
	1 hour		

Soak the garbanzo beans overnight in enough cold water to cover them and leave room for expansion. Drain the garbanzo beans and boil in fresh water until tender—about 1 hour. Drain.

To make the hummus, put the garbanzo beans into a food processor and blend with enough lemon juice and water to make a thick, smooth purée.

Add the garlic cloves. Mix well. Add the tahini and salt to taste. Add more lemon juice or water if necessary to get the flavor and consistency that you want.

Spoon into a serving dish, then drizzle over the olive oil and sprinkle with either cayenne or paprika. Garnish with the chopped parsley or cilantro.

Cover with plastic wrap and chill for 1 hour before serving.

taramasalata

		ingredients	
very easy		2 slices of white bread	pinch of cayenne pepper
		milk, to soak	3–6 tbsp lemon juice
serves 4		$2\frac{3}{4}$ oz/75 g smoked cod's roe	2–4 tbsp oil
		1 garlic clove, crushed	
10 minutes			
—			

Remove the crusts from the bread and soak in the milk for about 5 minutes, or until soft. Squeeze dry, reserving the liquid.

Combine the cod's roe, bread, garlic, and cayenne in a food processor and blend until smooth. Slowly add the lemon juice and oil, tasting frequently. Add the milk that was used to soak the bread if the consistency is not quite smooth enough.

Transfer the taramasalata to a serving dish. If not using immediately, cover with plastic wrap and refrigerate until 30 minutes before you need it.

sesame eggplant dip

		ingredients	
	very easy	1 medium eggplant	4–6 tbsp tahini
		4–6 tbsp olive oil	1–2 garlic cloves, crushed
	serves 4	juice of 1–2 lemons	1 tsp sesame seeds, to garnish
	10 minutes		
	15 minutes		

Place the eggplant on a preheated griddle or under the broiler and cook, turning frequently, until the skin is black and blistered. The eggplant itself will be very soft.

Transfer to a cutting board and let cool slightly. Cut it in half and scoop out the inside into a mixing bowl. Mash with a fork to make a coarse paste.

Gradually add the olive oil, lemon juice, tahini, and garlic. Mix well, tasting until you achieve the flavor and texture you like.

Transfer the mixture to an attractive bowl and serve at room temperature. If not using immediately, cover with plastic wrap and refrigerate until 30 minutes before you need it.

Just before serving, toss the sesame seeds in a very hot, dry skillet for a few seconds to toast them. Sprinkle over the eggplant spread to garnish.

guacamole

		ingredients	
	very easy	2 ripe avocados	2 tbsp fresh cilantro, chopped finely
		1 tomato	1 tbsp fresh red or green chile, seeded
	serves 4	juice of 1 lime	and chopped finely (optional)
		1 tbsp sweet onion, chopped finely	
	10 minutes		
	—		

Cut the avocados in half and discard the pits, then scoop the pulp into a large bowl. Mash to make a coarse paste.

Cut the tomato in half and remove all the seeds. Dice the flesh and add to the avocados.

Stir in the lime juice to loosen the mixture slightly, then stir in the onion, cilantro, and chile. Spoon into an attractive bowl and serve immediately.

vegetable cream dip

		ingredients	
	very easy	1 cup cream cheese	1 tbsp fresh parsley, chopped finely
		½ cup plain yogurt	1 tbsp fresh thyme, chopped finely
	serves 4	or sour cream	2 scallions, chopped finely
	5 minutes		
	—		

Beat the cream cheese in a large mixing bowl until it is soft and smooth.

Add the yogurt (or sour cream, if using), herbs, and one scallion. Mix well.

Cover with plastic wrap and refrigerate for at least 30 minutes. Stir thoroughly before transferring to a serving dish.

Sprinkle the remaining scallion over the top of the dip to garnish before serving.

smoked fish pâté

		ingredients	
	extremely easy	12 oz/350 g smoked mackerel, skinned and boned	3 tbsp lemon juice
			salt and pepper
	serves 4	¾ cup butter, melted	pinch of cayenne pepper
		½ cup heavy cream	
	10 minutes + at least 1 hour to chill		
	—		

Put the fish into a food processor and blend with half of the melted butter to a smooth paste.

Transfer the mixture into a bowl and gradually add the remaining butter, along with the cream and lemon juice, and season to taste.

Spoon into a serving dish and sprinkle with cayenne pepper.

Cover with plastic wrap and chill for at least 1 hour before serving.

easy onion dip

		ingredients
	extremely easy	1 cup sour cream
	serves 4	3 tbsp dried onion flakes
	5 minutes + at least 30 minutes to chill	2 beef bouillon cubes, crumbled
	—	

Combine the ingredients in a small bowl and mix very well.

Cover with plastic wrap and refrigerate for at least 30 minutes.

Stir thoroughly before transferring to a serving dish.

grandma's chopped herring

		ingredients
very easy		4 rollmops, with onions
		2 hard-cooked eggs
serves 4		1 cooking apple
		1 tbsp matzoh meal
		or fine bread crumbs
10 minutes		
—		

Skin the rollmops and chop with the onions, eggs, and apple.

Mix in the matzoh meal and turn into a serving dish. If not using immediately, cover with plastic wrap and refrigerate until 10 minutes before you need it.

new york
chopped liver

		ingredients
easy		3 tbsp chicken fat, diced
		1 onion, chopped finely
serves 4		8 oz/225 g chicken livers
		2 hard-cooked eggs
10 minutes		salt and pepper
10 minutes		

Place the chicken fat and 1 tablespoon of the onion in a skillet. Cook over a medium heat until the fat has melted and the remaining bits are very brown and crisp. Drain the crispy bits and set aside.

Sauté the chicken livers and the rest of the onion, chopped coarsely, in the hot chicken fat.

Drain the liver carefully, reserving the fat. Cool for a few minutes, then chop finely or grind, along with the onion and eggs. If you use a food processor, do not let the mixture get too smooth.

Spoon the liver mixture into a bowl and season to taste. Stir in the reserved crisp onions and just enough of the liquid chicken fat to bind. Transfer to a serving dish, then cover with plastic wrap and refrigerate until 10 minutes before serving.

cheese ball assortment

very easy	
serves 4	
20 minutes + 1 hour to chill	
—	

ingredients

BLUE CHEESE BALLS
- ½ cup blue cheese, crumbled
- ½ cup sour cream
- 2 tbsp scallions or chives, chopped finely
- 1 tbsp finely chopped celery

CREAM CHEESE BALLS
- ½ cup farmhouse cheese (eg Cheddar, Lancashire), grated
- scant ⅓ cup cream cheese
- 3 tbsp dry sherry or Martini
- few drops of Worcestershire sauce
- 2 tbsp scallions or chives, chopped finely
- 1 tbsp finely chopped celery

FETA CHEESE BALLS
- ½ cup Feta cheese, crumbled
- ½ cup butter, softened
- ½ tsp paprika
- 2 tbsp finely chopped fresh herbs

To make the blue cheese balls, mash the cheese and mix with the sour cream to make a smooth paste. Add the scallions and celery. With wet hands, take small spoonfuls of the mixture and form into balls. Arrange on a plate, cover with plastic wrap and then chill.

To make the cream cheese balls, mash the farmhouse cheese with the cream cheese to make a smooth paste. Season with sherry or Martini and with Worcestershire sauce. Fold in the scallions and celery. Shape and chill as above.

To make the feta cheese balls, mash the cheese with the butter to make a smooth paste. Season with paprika and herbs, then shape and chill as above.

The balls can be rolled in chopped nuts, shredded ham, ground green or red bell pepper, celery, or fresh herbs. A platter of assorted coatings makes a delicious and attractive hors d'œuvre.

stuffed vegetables

Stuffed vegetables can be eaten hot or cold, raw or cooked, filled with any combination of ingredients that you have available or that inspire you. Try serving Stuffed Mushrooms or Celery with Olive Cheese Filling as elegant hors d'œuvre or canapés for a drinks or dinner party. And Stuffed Tomatoes and Stuffed Bell Peppers make excellent picnic or lunch box snacks. They can even be used as a main course for a summer lunch or supper. Sauces for dipping can be added to provide that extra little something—turning a quick dish into a firm favorite.

stuffed mushrooms

	very easy	**ingredients**
	serves 4	1 lb/450 g white mushrooms 2 tbsp ground onion 3 garlic cloves ¾ cup butter
	15 minutes	
	20 minutes	

ingredients

1 lb/450 g white mushrooms
2 tbsp ground onion
3 garlic cloves
¾ cup butter

½ cup fresh white bread crumbs
1 tsp chopped fresh parsley
1 tbsp grated Parmesan cheese

Preheat the oven to 350°F/180°C.

Remove the mushroom stems and chop finely. Mix with the onion and 2 finely chopped cloves of garlic.

Melt half of the butter over a medium heat in a heavy skillet. Cook the mushroom stems, onion, and garlic for 3 minutes, or until softened. In a small bowl, combine the bread crumbs, parsley, and cheese. Stir into the hot onion mixture. Place a small spoonful in each mushroom cap.

Melt the remaining butter in a small pan. Grind the remaining garlic clove and toss in the butter for 2 minutes. Pour half into a shallow ovenproof dish.

Arrange the stuffed mushroom caps in the dish, then pour over the remaining butter and place the dish in the oven. Bake for 20 minutes. Serve hot.

stuffed tomatoes

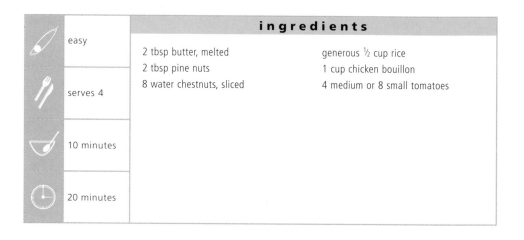

		ingredients	
easy		2 tbsp butter, melted	generous ½ cup rice
serves 4		2 tbsp pine nuts	1 cup chicken bouillon
10 minutes		8 water chestnuts, sliced	4 medium or 8 small tomatoes
20 minutes			

Melt the butter in a medium-sized pan over a medium heat. Toss in the pine nuts, water chestnuts, and rice. Stir to coat. Add the bouillon, then cover and cook gently for about 20 minutes, or until all the liquid is absorbed and the rice is soft. Let cool.

Slice the top off the tomatoes and scoop out the seeds. Fill with the cooked rice mixture and serve at room temperature.

stuffed bell peppers

		ingredients
	very easy	4 red, yellow, or green bell peppers
	serves 4	½ cup cream cheese ½ tsp lemon juice ½ cup smoked salmon, diced salt and pepper
	15 minutes + 3–4 hours to chill	
	—	

Cut a thick slice off the top of the bell peppers and carefully remove all the seeds.

Beat the cream cheese with the lemon juice until light and smooth. Add the diced salmon and blend thoroughly. Season to taste with salt and pepper.

Fill the bell peppers with cheese, packing it in gently. Cover with plastic wrap and chill for 3–4 hours.

To serve the bell peppers, unwrap them and cut into thin slices horizontally. Arrange overlapping slices on an attractive platter.

celery with olive
cheese filling

		ingredients	
very easy	12 celery stalks	2 scallions, chopped finely
	1 cup cream cheese	1 tbsp finely chopped fresh parsley
serves 4	½ cup black or green olives, pitted and chopped finely	2 tsp Tabasco or hot pepper sauce, optional
10 minutes	½ cup pimiento, chopped finely	
—		

Trim the celery stalks, removing the leaves and any rough strings.

Beat the cream cheese in a mixing bowl until soft and smooth.
Add all the other ingredients and mix well.

Spoon or pipe the cream cheese into the celery stalks. Cut
the stalks into 2 inch/5 cm pieces and arrange on an attractive
serving dish.

pastries
& toasties

There are as many different pastries and breads to choose from—plain or flavored, short or flaky, crusty or soft—as ways in which to use them. The recipes that follow should set your creative juices flowing—Miniature Onion Pizzas, Feta & Tomato Triangles, Olive & Tomato Bruschetta, or Broccoli Cashew Tarts. Experiment with these and invent your own alternatives for delicious treats at any time of the day.

cheese straws

		ingredients
very easy		flour, to roll out
serves 4		8 oz/225 g puff pastry 2 tsp mustard, optional
5 minutes		1 cup grated cheese cayenne pepper, optional
10 minutes		

Preheat the oven to 400°F/200°C.

Sprinkle your work surface with flour, then roll out the pastry to make a large rectangle.

Spread the mustard, cheese, and cayenne (if using) over the pastry, then cut it into thin strips about 4 inches/10 cm long.

Carefully arrange the straws on a greased cookie sheet, then transfer to the oven and bake for 5–10 minutes, or until crisp and golden.

Remove from the oven and let cool, then serve in baskets or piled high on plates.

specialty bread crisps

very easy		**ingredients**	
serves 4		4 pita bread or bagels, cut into thin slices horizontally 2 tbsp olive oil or melted butter	TOPPINGS 1 tsp black onion, dill, cumin, or crushed coriander seeds (optional) 1 tsp fresh rosemary, chopped (optional) 1 tsp sea salt (optional) 2 garlic cloves, chopped finely (optional)
5 minutes			
5 minutes			

Preheat the oven to 400°F/200°C.

Brush the pita bread with oil or butter and sprinkle with whichever toppings you have decided to use.

Arrange the bread on a cookie sheet and heat in the oven for 5 minutes, or until crispy and golden. Remove from the oven, then cut into fingers or triangles and serve immediately with a selection of Dips & Spreads (see pages 6–27).

miniature onion pizzas

		ingredients	
	very easy	¾ cup white bread flour, plus flour for kneading	TOPPING
	serves 4	½ tsp active dry yeast	4 tbsp olive oil
		½ tsp salt	1 large onion, sliced thinly
		1 tbsp olive oil	1 tsp brown sugar
	1¼ hours	½–1 cup warm water	1 tsp balsamic vinegar
			½ cup feta, mozzarella, or Gorgonzola cheese, grated or sliced
	10 minutes		

Mix the flour, yeast, and salt in a bowl. Drizzle over half of the oil. Make a well in the flour and pour in the water. Mix to a firm ball of dough. Turn it out onto a floured work surface and knead until no longer sticky. Add more flour if necessary. Grease the bowl with the remaining oil. Return the dough to the bowl, turn once to coat, then cover with a clean dish towel and let rise for 1 hour.

Heat the oil for the topping in a pan over a medium heat. Add the onion and cook for 10 minutes. Sprinkle with sugar and cook for 5 minutes more, stirring occasionally. Add the vinegar and cook for 5 more minutes. Remove from the heat and let cool.

Preheat the oven to 425°F/220°C. When the dough has doubled, punch it down to release excess air and knead until smooth, then divide into fourths and roll out to make thin circles. Place the dough on a cookie sheet, then spread with onions and top with cheese. Bake for 10 minutes. Remove from the oven and serve.

spinach, feta & tomato triangles

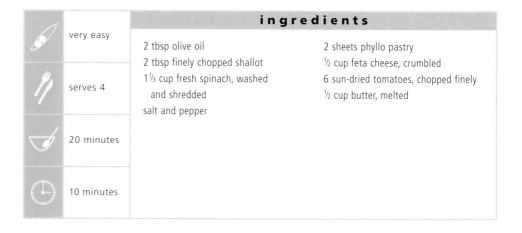

		ingredients
very easy	2 tbsp olive oil	2 sheets phyllo pastry
	2 tbsp finely chopped shallot	½ cup feta cheese, crumbled
serves 4	1⅓ cup fresh spinach, washed	6 sun-dried tomatoes, chopped finely
	and shredded	½ cup butter, melted
	salt and pepper	
20 minutes		
10 minutes		

Preheat the oven to 400°F/200°C. Heat the oil in a skillet over a medium heat and cook the shallot for 2–3 minutes. Add the spinach, then increase the heat to high and cook, stirring constantly, for 2–3 minutes. Remove from the heat and drain. Chop coarsely, then season to taste and let cool.

Cut each sheet of pastry into 6 strips. Place a spoonful of spinach at the bottom of each strip. Scatter cheese and tomatoes on top. Fold the bottom right-hand corner of each strip up to meet the opposite side to form a triangle. Fold the triangle toward the top of the strip and repeat until you reach the top of the strip.

Brush the edges of each triangle with melted butter, then transfer to a greased cookie sheet. Brush the top of the parcel with more butter. Place the cookie sheet in the oven and bake for 10 minutes, or until the pastry is golden and crispy. Remove from the oven and serve at once.

olive & tomato
bruschetta

		ingredients	
	very easy	½ cup extra-virgin olive oil	6 leaves fresh basil, torn
		1 small oval-shaped loaf of white	salt and pepper
	serves 4	bread (ciabatta or bloomer),	8 black olives, pitted and chopped
		cut into ½ inch/1 cm slices	1 large garlic clove, peeled and halved
	10 minutes	4 tomatoes, seeded and diced	
	5 minutes		

Pour half of the oil into a shallow dish and place the bread in it. Let stand for 1–2 minutes, then turn and let stand for another 2 minutes. The bread should be thoroughly saturated in oil.

Meanwhile, put the tomatoes in a mixing bowl. Sprinkle the basil leaves over the tomatoes. Season to taste with salt and pepper. Add the olives. Pour over the remaining olive oil and let marinate while you toast the bruschetta.

Preheat the broiler to medium. Place the bread on the broiler rack and cook until golden and crispy—about 2 minutes on each side.

Remove the bread from the broiler and arrange on a serving dish.

Rub the cut edge of the garlic halves over the surface of the bruschetta, then top each slice with a spoonful of the tomato mixture. Serve as soon as possible.

goat cheese
& chive croûtons

		ingredients
	very easy	½ cup extra-virgin olive oil
		8 x ½ inch/1 cm thick slices of
	serves 4	baguette or ciabatta
		4 oz/115 g goat cheese
		black pepper
	5 minutes	1 tbsp fresh chives, snipped finely
	10 minutes	

Pour the oil into a shallow dish and place the bread in it. Let stand for 1–2 minutes, then turn and let stand for an additional 2 minutes. The bread should be thoroughly saturated in oil.

Meanwhile, if the cheese has come in a log, cut into 8 slices. If it has come in rounds, crumble coarsely.

Preheat the oven to 350°F/180°C. Place the bread on a cookie sheet in the oven for 5 minutes. Remove the tray from the oven, then turn the bread over and top each slice with cheese. Sprinkle generously with black pepper.

Return the tray to the oven for another 5 minutes to heat the cheese thoroughly. Remove from the oven, then arrange the croûtons on plates and sprinkle with chives. Serve immediately.

broccoli cashew tart

		ingredients	
	very easy	8 oz/225 g unsweetened or cheese pastry	¾ cup cheese (eg, Cheddar, Emmenthal, Parmesan, Gruyère), grated coarsely
	serves 6–8	1 large head broccoli, cut into florets ½ cup unsalted cashew nuts, chopped ¼ cup butter	salt and pepper 1 egg
	45 minutes	⅓ cup all-purpose flour ¼ cup milk	pinch of cayenne pepper
	25 minutes		

Preheat the oven to 400°F/200°C. Roll out the pastry on a lightly floured surface and line a 9 inch/23 cm shallow pie dish and bake blind. Remove from the oven and let cool.

Steam the broccoli for 5 minutes. Remove and chop coarsely. Spread over the pastry case. Season, then sprinkle with nuts.

Melt the butter in a pan over a medium heat. Stir in the flour. Gradually add the milk, stirring, until the sauce has thickened. Season to taste. Add the grated cheese and cook until melted.

Separate the egg. Stir 2 tablespoons of cheese sauce into the yolk, then add to the sauce and mix. Remove from the heat. Whisk the egg white until stiff. Fold into the cheese sauce. Pour the sauce over the broccoli and spread gently. Sprinkle with cayenne pepper. Place the dish on a baking tray and bake for 20 minutes. Remove from the oven and let stand for 5 minutes before cutting.

spinach & potato puff

		ingredients	
very easy		12 oz/350 g small new potatoes, cooked, peeled, and cut into thick slices	½ tsp finely grated nutmeg
serves 4		12 oz/350 g puff pastry	8 oz/225 g mozzarella cheese, sliced or grated
25 minutes		flour, to roll out	salt and pepper
		1 lb/450 g fresh spinach or Swiss chard, washed thoroughly	1 egg
30 minutes			1 tbsp water

Prepare the potatoes and set aside. Cut the pastry into two pieces, one twice as large as the other. Roll the pastry out on a floured surface and trim into 2 rectangles. Keep the trimmings and let the pastry rest for 10 minutes.

Cook the spinach in a pan over a medium heat for 3–4 minutes. Drain, then chop and season with salt, pepper, and nutmeg.

Arrange a layer of potatoes on the larger rectangle, leaving a margin of pastry on all sides. Season to taste. Spread the spinach over the potatoes. Top with cheese and a final layer of potatoes.

Beat the egg and stir in the water. Fold the margins of the pastry to the center. Brush with egg. Put the smaller rectangle on top and seal. Transfer to a greased cookie sheet. Brush with egg. Roll out the trimmings and cut into shapes. Place on top of the pastry parcel and brush with egg. Bake for 30 minutes. Remove from the oven. Let stand for 5 minutes before slicing and serving.

basil zucchini
toasties

		ingredients	
easy		4 slices of white bread	1 cup grated cheese
		¼ cup butter, melted	1 cup fresh bread crumbs
serves 4		4 eggs	1 tbsp finely chopped fresh basil
		2 cups milk	salt and pepper
		1 small onion, chopped finely	pinch of paprika
10 minutes		1 zucchini, grated	2 tbsp Parmesan cheese, grated
45 minutes			

Preheat the oven to 375°F/190°C.

Remove the crusts from the bread and press them into the cups of a muffin pan. Brush well with melted butter.

Beat the eggs well in a medium-sized mixing bowl. Stir in the milk. Add the onion, zucchini, cheese, crumbs, basil, and seasoning. Mix well.

Carefully pour the egg mixture into the bread cases. Sprinkle with the paprika and Parmesan cheese, then place the pan in the oven and bake for about 45 minutes, or until set and golden.

Turn off the oven, but let the toasties cool for 10 minutes before transferring to a serving platter.

nibbles

These are the small dishes, appropriate for any party food occasion, but not meals in themselves unless made in larger quantities or, better yet, served with a host of companion nibbles. Mix and match them, make some hot and some cold, and offer them with a selection of bread, crisps, raw vegetables, and sauces for dipping. Let your imagination go wild and have a tasty time.

bite-size barbecued
spare ribs

easy	
serves 4	
10 minutes	
20 minutes	

ingredients

SAUCE
¼ cup plum, hoisin, sweet
  & sour, or duck sauce
1 tsp brown sugar
1 tbsp tomato ketchup
pinch of garlic powder
2 tbsp dark soy sauce

2 lb 4 oz/1 kg spare ribs, chopped
  into 2 inch/5 cm pieces

3 tbsp fresh, torn cilantro, to garnish

Preheat the oven to 375°F/190°C.

To make the sauce, combine the plum or other sauce, brown sugar, ketchup, garlic powder, and soy sauce in a large mixing bowl.

Add the spare ribs to the sauce and stir to coat them thoroughly. Transfer to a metal roasting pan and arrange in a single layer.

Place the roasting pan in the oven and cook the ribs for 20 minutes, or until they are cooked through and sticky. Arrange on a large platter and serve immediately, garnished with cilantro.

devilled eggs

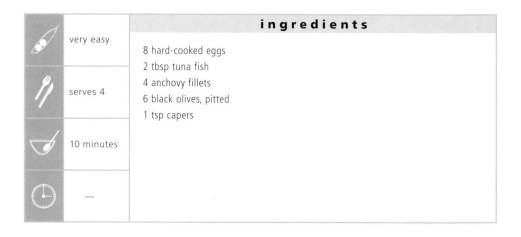

		ingredients		
	very easy	8 hard-cooked eggs		
	serves 4	2 tbsp tuna fish		
		4 anchovy fillets		
	10 minutes	6 black olives, pitted		
	—	1 tsp capers		

Peel the eggs, then cut in half lengthwise and remove the yolks. Mash the yolks, or put in the food processor, along with the tuna, 2 anchovies, 4 olives, and all of the capers.

Blend the ingredients together to make a smooth paste, adding 1 teaspoon of oil from the tuna or anchovies, or some extra-virgin olive oil, to achieve the correct consistency.

Arrange the egg whites on an attractive serving dish. Fill the gaps with the yolk mixture, using either a teaspoon or a piping bag. Make sure the filling is piled high.

Garnish the filled eggs with the remaining anchovies and olives (cut into tiny strips) and serve.

fresh figs
with gorgonzola

very easy	**ingredients**
serves 4	8 slices baguette, ciabatta or bloomer ½ cup Gorgonzola or other strong blue cheese, sliced or crumbled 4 fresh figs, sliced thinly
5 minutes	
8–10 minutes	

Preheat the broiler. Place the bread on the broiler pan and toast until golden on one side. Remove the pan.

Turn the bread over and sprinkle with cheese, making sure that it covers each slice right to the edge.

Arrange the figs on top of the cheese.

Return the pan to the broiler and cook for 3–4 minutes, or until the cheese is soft and the fruit is hot. Transfer to an attractive dish and serve immediately.

chorizo & olive frittata

		ingredients	
easy		¼ cup butter	8 large eggs
		1 small onion, chopped finely	2 tbsp milk
serves 4		1 small green or red bell pepper, seeded and chopped finely	salt and pepper
			½ cup Cheddar cheese, grated
		2 tomatoes, seeded and diced	
10 minutes		2 small cooked potatoes, diced	GARNISH
		125 g/4½ oz chorizo or salami, chopped finely	mixed salad leaves
			pimiento strips
15 minutes		8 green or black olives, pitted and chopped finely	

Melt the butter over a medium heat in a large skillet. Add the onion, bell pepper, and tomatoes. Stir well to coat in butter, then cook for 3–4 minutes, or until soft. Mix in the potatoes, chorizo, and olives. Cook gently for 5 minutes to heat through.

In a small bowl, beat the eggs with the milk, salt, and pepper. Pour over the vegetables in the skillet and reduce the heat to low. Cook the eggs, occasionally lifting the edges and tilting the skillet to let the liquid run to the outside.

Preheat the broiler to high. When the eggs are mostly set, with only a small wet patch in the middle, sprinkle over the cheese. Place the skillet under the broiler and cook for 2 minutes, or until the cheese has melted and is golden brown. Remove the skillet from the broiler and let the fritatta cool before cutting into wedges. Garnish with salad leaves and pimiento and serve.

falafel

		ingredients	
easy		2 cups dried garbanzo beans cold water, to cover	½ tsp baking powder oil, for deep frying
serves 4		1 large onion, chopped finely 1 garlic clove, crushed salt	SERVING SUGGESTIONS hummus (see page 8)
1 hour + 1 hour to rest		cayenne pepper 2 tbsp chopped fresh parsley 2 tsp ground cumin	sesame eggplant dip (see page 12) pita bread tomato wedges
25 minutes – 1 hour 10 minutes		2 tsp ground coriander	

Soak the garbanzo beans overnight in enough cold water to cover them and leave room for expansion. Drain the garbanzo beans and boil in fresh water until tender, about 1 hour (or 15 minutes, if using a pressure cooker). Drain.

To make the falafel, put the garbanzo beans into a food processor and blend to make a coarse paste. Add the onion, garlic, seasoning, and baking powder and blend again to mix thoroughly.

Let the mixture rest for 30 minutes, then shape into 8 patties and arrange on a plate. Let rest for another 30 minutes.

Heat the oil in a wok or deep skillet. Gently drop in the patties and cook until golden brown. Carefully remove from the oil and drain for a few minutes on a plate lined with paper towels.

Serve hot or at room temperature with a selection of dips, accompanied by tomato wedges or sandwiched into pita bread.

cheesy corn puffs

		ingredients

easy	¼ cup butter
	⅔ cup water
	scant ⅔ cup all-purpose flour mixed
	  with salt and pepper
	1 egg
		pinch of cayenne pepper or chili
		  powder (optional)
		¼ cup grated cheese
		  (eg, Emmenthal, Gruyère, Cheddar)
		1 tbsp corn, fried onion,
		  cooked mushrooms, or diced ham
		oil, for deep frying

easy

serves 4

15 minutes

10 minutes

To make the choux pastry, place the butter and water in a small pan. Heat until the water boils, then remove from the heat. Add the seasoned flour immediately and mix well until it forms a ball that leaves the side of the pan clean. Beat in the egg, a little bit at a time, until it has all been absorbed.

Season the pastry with cayenne (if using) and stir in the cheese and whichever flavorings you choose.

Heat the oil in a wok or deep skillet. Gently drop small spoonfuls of the pastry into the oil. Cook until golden brown and well puffed. Carefully remove from the oil and drain for a few minutes on a plate lined with paper towels. Serve immediately.

miniature chicken kabobs

easy	
serves 4	
15 minutes + 30 minutes to marinate	
10 minutes	

ingredients

SWEET & SOUR MARINADE
½ cup orange, grapefruit,
  or pineapple juice
1 tbsp sweet sherry
¼ cup dark soy sauce
¼ cup chicken bouillon
2 tbsp cider vinegar
1 tsp tomato paste
2 tbsp light brown sugar
pinch of ground ginger

1 chicken breast, skinned, boned and
  cut into ½ inch/1 cm pieces
½ small onion, cut into
  ½ inch/1 cm pieces
½ red bell pepper, cut into
  ½ inch/1 cm pieces
½ green bell pepper, cut into
  ½ inch/1 cm pieces

To make the marinade, combine all the liquid ingredients in a mixing bowl. Add the tomato paste, sugar, and ginger. Mix well, then add the chicken and vegetables and stir to coat thoroughly.

Cover the bowl with plastic wrap and place in the refrigerator to marinate for 30 minutes.

Drain off the marinade and reserve. Place alternating pieces of chicken and vegetables on toothpicks, taking care not to pack them too tightly together.

Preheat a griddle or heavy skillet over a high heat. Place the kabobs in the skillet and cook, turning frequently, for about 10 minutes, or until gently browned and cooked through. Baste occasionally with the reserved marinade.

Pile the kabobs high on platters and serve immediately.

miniature
beef kabobs

easy

serves 4

10 minutes
+ 30 minutes
to marinate

5 minutes

ingredients

SPICY TOMATO MARINADE
¼ cup tomato juice
¼ cup beef bouillon
1 tbsp Worcestershire sauce
1 tbsp lemon juice
2 tbsp dry sherry
few drops of Tabasco sauce
2 tbsp vegetable oil
1 tbsp ground celery

115 g/4 oz sirloin or rump steak, cut
  into cubes about ½ inch/1 cm in size
4 white mushrooms, cut into cubes
  about ½ inch/1 cm in size
½ small onion, cut into cubes about
  ½ inch/1 cm in size

Combine all the ingredients for the marinade in a large mixing bowl and whisk well, then stir in the meat, mushrooms, and onion. Cover the bowl with plastic wrap and place in the refrigerator to marinate for 30 minutes.

Drain off the marinade and reserve. Place alternating pieces of steak and vegetables on toothpicks, taking care not to pack them too tightly together.

Preheat a griddle or heavy skillet over a high heat. Place the kabobs in the skillet and cook, turning frequently, until gently browned and cooked through—about 5 minutes. Baste occasionally with the reserved marinade.

Pile the kabobs high on platters and serve immediately.

mixed vegetable fritters

		ingredients	
easy		BATTER	1 large sweet onion, sliced thickly,
		scant 1¼ cups all-purpose flour	rings separated
		½ tsp baking powder	1 large zucchini, cut into batons
serves 4		pinch of salt	1 small eggplant, cut into batons
		1 egg	1 small cauliflower, cut into florets
		½ cup milk	4 oz/115 g white mushrooms,
15 minutes		½ tsp Tabasco sauce	stems trimmed off level with caps
		(optional)	
			lemon wedges, to garnish
15 minutes		oil, for deep frying	garlicky tomato sauce, to serve

To prepare the batter, combine the dry ingredients in a large mixing bowl. Add the egg, beating to eliminate lumps. Gradually add the milk, stirring constantly. Add Tabasco sauce (if using).

Heat the oil in a wok or deep skillet. Dip the vegetables into the batter, then lift out and let any excess drip back into the bowl. Gently drop into the wok and cook until golden brown. Carefully remove from the oil and drain for a few minutes on a plate lined with paper towels.

Serve hot, garnished with lemon wedges or accompanied by a garlicky tomato sauce for dipping.

parsley fish balls

easy	
serves 4	
10 minutes	
15 minutes	

ingredients

1 lb/450 g white fish fillets, skinned
and cut into large chunks
1 onion, cut into fourths
2 eggs
4 tbsp matzoh meal or bread crumbs
salt and pepper
1 tbsp finely chopped fresh parsley

oil, for deep frying

sweet and sour or chili dipping sauce,
to serve

Place the fish and onion in a food processor. Blend to make a coarse paste, then put the paste into a large mixing bowl.

Add the eggs and matzoh meal (or bread crumbs, if using) and stir to bind. Season with salt, pepper, and parsley.

Heat the oil in a wok or deep skillet.

Shape the fish into small balls or patties and gently drop into the oil. Cook until golden brown. Carefully remove from the oil and drain for a few minutes on a plate lined with paper towels.

Serve the fish hot or at room temperature, accompanied by sweet and sour or chili sauce for dipping.

shrimp balls

very easy	
serves 4	
5 minutes + 30 minutes to chill	
10 minutes	

ingredients

1 lb/450 g shrimp	½ tsp salt
6–10 water chestnuts	oil, for deep frying
1 tbsp ground onion	
1 tsp finely grated fresh ginger	sweet and sour, chili, or sweet soy
1 egg, beaten	sauce, to serve
2 tbsp cornstarch	
1 tbsp dry sherry	lemon slices, to garnish

Put the shrimp, water chestnuts, onion, and ginger in a food processor and blend to make a thick paste. Transfer to a mixing bowl and add the egg, cornstarch, sherry, and salt. Mix well. Cover the bowl with plastic wrap and chill for 30 minutes.

Meanwhile, shape the shrimp paste into small balls. Heat the oil in a wok or deep skillet. Drop the balls gently into the oil and cook until golden brown. Carefully remove from the oil and drain for a few minutes on a plate lined with paper towels.

Serve the shrimp balls hot with a sweet and sour, chili, or sweet soy sauce for dipping or garnished lemon slices.

buttered herby
new potatoes

		ingredients
	extremely easy	12 small new potatoes
		½ cup butter
	serves 4	2 tbsp finely ground fresh rosemary
		salt and pepper
	10 minutes	
	20 minutes	

Boil the potatoes in salted water until just tender. Drain well.

Melt the butter in a large, heavy skillet. Add the rosemary and the potatoes and mix well. Continue cooking, stirring frequently, for 5 minutes, or until the potatoes are thoroughly coated in rosemary butter and are starting to brown.

Arrange the potatoes on large platters, then sprinkle with salt and pepper and serve immediately.

savory rice balls

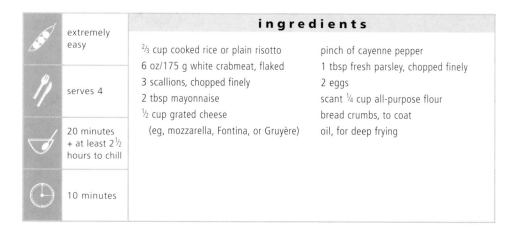

	ingredients	
extremely easy	⅔ cup cooked rice or plain risotto	pinch of cayenne pepper
	6 oz/175 g white crabmeat, flaked	1 tbsp fresh parsley, chopped finely
serves 4	3 scallions, chopped finely	2 eggs
	2 tbsp mayonnaise	scant ¼ cup all-purpose flour
	½ cup grated cheese	bread crumbs, to coat
20 minutes + at least 2½ hours to chill	(eg, mozzarella, Fontina, or Gruyère)	oil, for deep frying
10 minutes		

Combine the rice, crabmeat, scallions, mayonnaise, cheese, cayenne, parsley, and one egg in a large bowl. Mix well. Cover the bowl with plastic wrap and refrigerate for at least 2 hours, but overnight if possible.

Take spoonfuls of the mixture and roll, with wet hands, into small balls. Cover as before and chill for another 30 minutes.

Heat the oil over a high heat in a large wok or deep pan.

Meanwhile, beat the remaining egg. Gently roll the rice balls in flour, then quickly dip them in beaten egg. Coat thoroughly and drain off any excess.

Roll the rice balls in bread crumbs. Press the crumbs in firmly but gently, shake off any loose crumbs, then cook for about 5 minutes, or until crisp and golden. Drain well and serve either hot or cold.

crunchy potato skins

		ingredients
easy		4 potatoes, cooked in their skins
		2 strips of lean bacon
serves 4		½ cup blue cheese, crumbled
		oil, for deep frying
10 minutes		crème fraîche or sour cream, to garnish
5 minutes		

Cut the potatoes in half and scoop out the soft inside, leaving a lining about ¼ inch/5 mm thick.

Broil the bacon until crisp. Transfer to a plate and cut into small strips. Combine the blue cheese and bacon in a small mixing bowl.

Heat the oil over a high heat in a wok or deep skillet. Carefully drop the potato skins into the oil and cook for 3–4 minutes, or until crisp and golden. Remove and drain well on paper towels.

Arrange the potato skins on a large plate and fill each with a spoonful of the bacon and cheese mixture, piling it high so it is almost overflowing. Garnish with a teaspoon of crème fraîche or sour cream and serve immediately.

oven-fried
chicken wings

		ingredients	
very easy		12 chicken wings	1 tsp paprika
		1 egg	salt and pepper
serves 4		¼ cup milk	4 cups bread crumbs
		4 heaped tbsp all-purpose flour	¼ cup butter
15 minutes			
20 minutes			

Separate the chicken wings into 3 pieces each. Discard the bony tip. Beat the egg with the milk in a shallow dish. Combine the flour, paprika, salt, and pepper in a shallow dish. Place the bread crumbs in a shallow dish.

Preheat the oven to 425°F/220°C.

Dip the chicken pieces into the egg and coat well, then drain and dredge in flour. Remove, shaking off any excess, and roll in crumbs, pressing them in gently, then shaking off any excess.

Melt the butter in the oven in a shallow roasting pan large enough to hold all the chicken pieces in a single layer. Arrange the chicken, skin side down, in the butter and bake for 10 minutes. Turn and bake for an additional 10 minutes.

Remove the chicken from the pan and arrange on a large platter. Serve hot or at room temperature.

crispy bacon nibbles

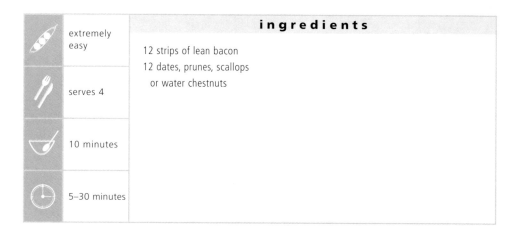

		ingredients
	extremely easy	12 strips of lean bacon
	serves 4	12 dates, prunes, scallops or water chestnuts
	10 minutes	
	5–30 minutes	

Holding the bacon down firmly with a knife or fork on a cutting board, use a sharp knife to smooth and stretch the length.

Place a date, scallop, or water chestnut at one end of each strip and roll up. Secure with a toothpick to keep it closed.

Preheat a ridged griddle or broiler until very hot. Place the bacon rolls on the griddle or on the broiler and cook, turning once, for 5–10 minutes, or until the bacon is crisp and well browned. Whatever is wrapped in the bacon must be thoroughly cooked or heated through. Alternatively, you could cook the bacon rolls on a flat cookie sheet for 25–30 minutes in an oven preheated to 400°F/200°C.

Transfer to a large platter and serve immediately.

ham & parmesan
pinwheels

		ingredients	
easy			
	1 small loaf of bread		4 slices of ham (plain, cured,
serves 4	4 tbsp butter, mustard, or		or smoked)
	cream cheese		4 tbsp grated Parmesan cheese
10 minutes			8 sun-dried tomatoes, optional
5 minutes			

Remove the crusts from the bread and cut into four slices
lengthwise. Place each slice between two pieces of waxed
paper and flatten with a rolling pin. Remove the paper.

Preheat the oven to 350°F/180°C.

Spread each slice of bread with butter, mustard, or cream cheese
and top with slices of ham. Sprinkle Parmesan cheese over the
top. If you are using sun-dried tomatoes, chop them and scatter
over the cheese.

Roll up the bread along its length, then cut into ½ inch/1 cm slices
crosswise. Place the pinwheels, cut side up, on a greased cookie
tray. Transfer to the oven and bake for 5 minutes, or until the
cheese has melted. Remove from the oven, then place on a dish
and serve either hot or cold.

hot salsa nachos

		ingredients	
extremely easy		2 packs of nachos or tortilla chips	TO SERVE
serves 4		4 tbsp jalapeño peppers, sliced finely	tomato salsa
5 minutes		1 cup Cheddar cheese, grated	guacamole
10 minutes			sour cream
		2 tbsp finely chopped fresh cilantro, to garnish	

Preheat the oven to 375°F/190°C.

Tip the nachos into a shallow ovenproof dish. Sprinkle with the peppers and top with the cheese. Bake for 5–10 minutes to melt the cheese.

Remove the nachos from the oven and garnish with cilantro, then serve with salsa, guacamole, and a dish of sour cream.

index